ARE YOU WORTH THE WAIT?

ARE YOU WORTH THE WAIT?

From Fledgling Editor to Sought-After Professional

By Susan Hughes

THE-EFA.ORG

Copyright © 2023 by Susan Hughes
Cover and design © 2023 Editorial Freelancers Association
New York, NY

All rights reserved.

No part of this publication may be reproduced, distributed, or transmitted in any form or by any means, including, but not limited to, photocopying, recording, or other electronic or mechanical methods, without the prior written permission of the publisher, except in the case of brief quotations embodied in critical reviews and certain other noncommercial uses permitted by copyright law. For permission requests, write to the publisher at "Attention: Publications Chairperson," at the address below.

266 West 37th St., 20th Floor
New York, NY 10018
info@the-efa.org

ISBN paperback   978-1-880407-52-3
ISBN ebook   978-1-880407-53-0

Hughes, Susan. *Are You Worth the Wait? From Fledgling Editor to Sought-After Professional*
An EFA Booklet: Published in the United States of America by the Editorial Freelancers Association.

Subject Categories: Editing & Proofreading | Communication Studies | Business Skills

Legal Disclaimer

While the publisher and author have made every attempt to verify that the information provided in this book is correct and up to date, the publisher and author assume no responsibility for any error, inaccuracy, or omission.

The advice, examples, and strategies contained herein are not suitable for every situation. Neither the publisher nor author shall be liable for damages arising therefrom. This book is not intended for use as a source of legal or financial advice. Running a business involves complex legal and financial issues. You should always retain competent legal and financial professionals to provide guidance.

EFA Publications Chairperson: Robin Martin
Copyeditor: Tia Ross
Proofreader: Maria Alonzo
Book Designer: Stephanie Argy
Cover Designer: Robot House

See more by the author:
MyIndependentEditor.com myindependenteditor.com
Twitter @HughesEdits4U twitter.com/hughesedits4u
Facebook @MyIndependentEditor facebook.com/MyIndependentEditor
LinkedIn susan-hughes/5b/2a2/720 linkedin.com/pub/susan-hughes/5b/2a2/720
Instagram @susanhughes5876 instagram.com/susanhughes5876

Contents

Introduction	1
Are You Worth the Wait?	3
Know Your Stuff	3
Get Organized	4
Build Your Brand	5
Grow Your Social Media Presence	6
Ditch Your Ego	7
Communicate	8
Be Assertive, yet Mindful	9
Learn to Walk the Tightrope Between Serious Professional and "Real" Person	11
Teach Them What You Know	12
Surrender Your Role as Team Captain	14
So, Now What?	15
Charge What You're Worth	15
Don't Overbook	16
In Conclusion	17
About the Author	**18**

Introduction

When I launched my freelance editing business twelve years ago after retiring from a twenty-nine-year teaching career, I had no plan, no clear idea about what I was doing. I never realized that a new career was in the works. I had no clue that I would eventually be busy enough to have to schedule my clients in advance. Even further from my mind was the idea that writers would be willing to wait for my services—sometimes as long as six months!

In this booklet, I share what I learned in my journey to become a wait-worthy freelance editor. I must warn you that it's not a quick process. It takes time and dedication to reach the point where clients will pay to reserve editing time with you months before you're available to provide the services they're looking for. What follows worked for me, and it can work for you as well.

Are You Worth the Wait?

Know Your Stuff

If you haven't mastered the art of editing, none of the other suggestions in this booklet matter. And it is, indeed, an art. As an editor, your artwork begins not with a blank canvas but with a nearly completed picture—a story or article that has already been written and self-edited. It is your job to transform the piece into an error-free, easy-to-read masterpiece.

I've been blessed with a natural talent for writing and a keen eye for errors—yes, I'm obsessive about those commas—but I still frequently consult a variety of resources while I'm editing. I have online subscriptions to *The Chicago Manual of Style* and the *AP Stylebook*, and I switch back and forth between them, depending upon the requirements of the document I'm working on. I also have hard copies of these resources, but I find it handier to use the digital version. Additionally, I have easy-to-access copies of the latest versions of *The Merriam-Webster Dictionary* and the *Cambridge British English Dictionary*. I also keep the *Urban Dictionary* bookmarked. If I'm uncertain about something, I look it up. I do whatever it takes to get it right.

Staying up to date on the latest trends in editing is time consuming, but it's an absolute necessity. Writers need to feel confident that you aren't editing by some old-school standards that are no longer viable. *The Chicago Manual of Style* and the *AP Stylebook* frequently put out updates and make changes to their standards. If you have online subscriptions to them, you'll automatically be notified when they do so.

Building your skills and staying current on writing and editing trends might mean taking a class or two. The Editorial Freelancers

Association (EFA) offers a wide range of webinars and online courses that can serve as a refresher or provide you with new ideas and ways to increase your editing skill level. You can find them in the catalog on the organization's website, listed under the Education tab, or via this link: the-efa.org/education.

If you prefer something a bit less structured but want to keep up with the latest recommendations and changes in the editing world, join your local chapter of the EFA or other editorial organization, or find some podcasts to follow. There are great ones out there.

Regardless of which method you prefer when it comes to keeping abreast of the latest trends in writing and editing, if you're serious about being a wait-worthy freelancer, do whatever it takes to gain the skills and confidence you need to keep clients coming back for more. Put aside everything else and focus on learning the art itself.

Get Organized

Organization is crucial if you want to be a successful freelancer, and it becomes even more vital if you're booking clients several months in advance. Use a calendar app on your phone or computer to keep track of your editing jobs. If you're the pen-and-paper sort, purchase a day planner. Just be sure to have a pencil handy because booking in advance requires flexibility. Keep track of the fee you quote each client, how much deposit they pay upfront, if required, and any other specifics about your editing agreement. If you want clients to have enough confidence in you that they'll wait for your services, you have to stay on top of the little details. Consider using a contract for your work, and always be willing to provide one if the client requests it. The EFA provides sample contracts and letters of agreement on their website. the-efa.org/resources.

Build Your Brand

If potential clients are going to take you seriously—and they'll have to in order to have the courage to pay a deposit and wait for your services—you need to create and perfect your professional brand, which reflects your reputation as an editor. Much of this goes hand in hand with creating an online presence and building a social media following.

Start by building a website for your editing business. Potential clients will want to know more about you before investing in long-range editing. They'll connect with you and then want to check you out further before they're willing to wait for your services. You can build a simple website yourself using sites like WordPress or GoDaddy or invest in professional web design. Whatever you choose to do, be sure your website is attractive, has an easy-to-follow layout, and is free of errors. Stay focused on your editing business, including your rates, requirements, and other pertinent details. Look at my website and those of other successful editors to get ideas. I add a touch of the personal by including a bio and a few photographs in keeping with my belief that it's important that potential clients find you authentic. I'll discuss that in detail in a later section of this booklet.

Next, invest in a professional headshot. To build your brand, you need to be easily identified, so use the same professional photo in everything you do related to your editing business. Put it on your website, and use it as your profile photo on social media.

Once these pieces are in place, begin to share what you know about editing. Start a blog about editing or pen articles about writing, editing, publishing—any topic related to the industry. Add those to your website or post them online. No time to blog regularly? Find bloggers who will let you write guest posts or who are willing to interview you about your editing business. I've done both and have gained new clients from it. You can find a few examples under the In the Media tab on my website: myindependenteditor.com.

Offer writers a free sample edit to show them what you can do to improve their work. I ask new prospective clients to submit a 1,000-word sample via my website or by email, and then I edit it just like I would any other project. This gives me a preview of the writer's skill level and offers the prospective client a glimpse of what they will get if they hire me.

Branding takes time, but it will go a long way in providing the authenticity required to give clients the courage to wait for your services.

Grow Your Social Media Presence

Despite being a busy full-time freelancer, I make time for building my follower base on social media. It's a must in today's world. Working from home requires some creative networking skills, and social media provides that for me. I have a Facebook business page and am active on Twitter, LinkedIn, and Instagram. However, word-of-mouth referrals from satisfied clients generate the bulk of my new business.

While it's tempting to self-promote, successful social media marketing requires some restraint where that's concerned. I try to follow the 80-20 rule: 80 percent of my posts are about something other than me and my editing business. I spend most of my time sharing posts for others with whom I've connected. Potential clients need to feel that you are sincerely interested in them and their ideas.

Getting yourself to wait-worthy status takes time and effort—much more so than maintaining that level of credibility once you get there—but it's worth it.

Speaking of time . . . some of that can be minimized by using automated posting services. I use Social Jukebox to schedule posts to Twitter, Facebook, and LinkedIn. You can also cross-post to Instagram from your Facebook page. Like to make short videos to share? Maybe TikTok is the place for you. Whichever social media platform(s) you prefer, automating your posts leaves time for supporting others while still building your brand.

For those of you who prefer to steer clear of social media, there are marketers available to handle it for you. In using such a service, however, you miss out on the interaction and personal networking that lies at the very heart of social media.

Ditch Your Ego

So, you've worked hard to polish your editing skills, have a growing list of faithful followers on social media, and have focused on building your brand. It would be easy to sit back at this point and feel mighty proud of yourself. There's no time for that if you're intent upon becoming a wait-worthy freelancer. Now's the time to ditch your ego and set your sights on the long-term goal you've established for yourself.

No matter how good you are at polishing prose or how keen your eyes are when it comes to spotting the little errors that muddy up an otherwise marvelous manuscript, you have to be able to remain objective as you edit. The writer's voice must remain intact, even if your personal writing style is in direct conflict with it. Your personal biases and tastes have no place in the editing process. To inject those preferences into your clients' writing is to tell them they're not quite good enough. A skilled editor is able to spot flawless writing and be objective enough to say, "This is great! Wow! Congratulations on a job well done," if that is, indeed, the case. No need to add or adjust or move words around to make it more in keeping with your own writing style. It's not about you. A wait-worthy editor knows this.

Communicate

This topic comes up in almost all the feedback I receive from clients. Can you blame writers for wanting to work with someone with whom they can communicate in a professional, timely manner? There are thousands of freelance editors out there, and you can bet that most potential clients are querying a number of prospects. If you don't reply to their emails or online messages in a timely manner, you're going to miss out on their business before you even have a chance to prove your worth. Regardless of what format you use for communicating about your business—be it email, text, phone call, Messenger, Twitter, or something else—stay on top of it.

Prompt, professional communication is an ongoing part of the editor-client relationship. I communicate primarily via email once an edit begins. If it's a long project, such as a lengthy manuscript, I provide a weekly update to let the client know where things stand. I do this on Friday afternoon, and my clients have come to expect it. They appreciate knowing that I'm still out there somewhere, working diligently on their book or other project. In this digital world we live in, where we don't often sit face-to-face with our clients, it's even more important to establish that link.

Likewise, I make it known from the beginning that I'm open to questions, comments, and concerns—before, during, and after the edit. If a client has booked an edit four months in advance, I touch base with them each month prior to the edit. It doesn't have to be a long, drawn-out ordeal. A simple email works well to let the client know you're still on target with their editing start date.

Sometimes, however, email is not the client's preferred means of communication. In that case, I do whatever I can to make the client feel comfortable, be it texting, a phone call, or a conversation using Skype, FaceTime, or Messenger. While communication is key when it comes to establishing a strong client-editor relationship, it's important to gauge each new client's preference when it comes to contact.

Whatever you do, be sure to save all emails and document the date and important details of each call or chat in case you need to refer to them later.

Communication with clients doesn't end when the edit is complete. I make it a point to follow up with them in the weeks after the edit, assuring them that I'm available to answer questions or provide guidance as needed. For many writers, the post-edit revision period is a stressful part of the process, and clients have told me that they feel more confident knowing I'm still around to help if needed. Sometimes all they require is a word or two of reassurance. Ongoing communication helps the client feel more confident, both during the edit and after, knowing I'm there as a sounding board or simply as moral support.

I often receive emails from clients during the weekend. Writing and editing are not nine-to-five jobs. I check my email daily and reply promptly, regardless of what day it is. It's part of building that connection with clients that makes me worth the wait. Yes, it can be tedious and time-consuming, but consider your goal. Do you want to have so many clients that you have to book six months in advance to fit them in? Do you want writers to book an edit with you before they even finish the first draft of their manuscript? If your answer is yes, which I assume it is if you're still reading this, make prompt, professional, friendly communication a top priority. You'll be amazed at the difference it makes.

Be Assertive, yet Mindful

No writer wants a wishy-washy editor. You know what you're doing, so don't be afraid to do it. Tell your client when they're being too wordy or have drifted off topic or have repeated themselves too many times. Do your job with confidence. And while you're at it, learn how to read your clients. Know when to push harder and when to back off a bit. It's a delicate dance but one that will set you apart from the others once you master it. Be mindful enough to give your clients the confidence they need to write and rewrite boldly, whether it's a news article you're editing or a full-length piece of historical fiction.

As your assertiveness grows, so does your need for thicker skin. Writers are a sensitive bunch. If you've been editing for a while, you already know this. Criticism is tough to take, no matter what the situation, but it seems particularly difficult for writers. They've poured so much of themselves into their work, and the words on the page are held close to their heart. Then they hand it over to a stranger who proceeds to cut and chop and critique it nearly to death. You are going to hear about it, trust me. A wait-worthy editor knows not to take this personally and is mindful of the client's personal attachment to their work.

I have a client who was livid when I returned his edited manuscript, having cut nearly seventy pages of extraneous detail that was distracting from the story. He raged and wailed and emailed me a long, pain-filled letter. "How could you butcher my story like that?" he asked, obviously distressed at what I'd done. I replied in a professional manner, explaining for a second (or maybe a third) time why I cut out what I did. I suggested he give it a little time, let the manuscript rest for a bit, and then we could discuss it again if he wanted to. I told him I was sorry he was so distraught, but I did not apologize for the job I'd done. He emailed me two weeks later and apologized. "You were right," he said. "It was just difficult for me to accept it."

A week later he sent me flowers. His wife had told him he was too hard on me. We had a good laugh over it and have since become friends. As of this writing, I have edited five novels for him, and the sixth will be ready for editing later this year.

If you have great editing skills, are organized, assertive, and have skin as thick as an elephant's, you're ready to move your freelance editing job to the next level. What follows will help you get there.

Learn to Walk the Tightrope Between Serious Professional and "Real" Person

As a freelancer, much of your work will be done outside the traditional office setting. Face-to-face meetings with your clients will be a rarity, so it's more important than ever to build a brand that is viewed as both authentic and professional. If you want clients to feel comfortable and confident in you, enough so to book your services months in advance even though someone else might be available tomorrow, they must be able to connect with you as a person and have confidence in your professional ability.

I try to balance the two skillfully in my client communications. My emails and texts are friendly, positive, and professional. I pay close attention to what my clients tell me and am careful to follow up with them regarding things that might be going on in their lives. I recently had a client tell me about a health problem she was having. When I didn't hear from her for a couple of weeks, I sent a quick email to check on her progress. It's not hard to do, but it does take time. Time. There it is again. Remind yourself of your goal. Invest the time.

I also do my best balancing act when I'm on social media. I post meaningful quotes and newsworthy items—and yes, from time to time I toss in a cute animal photo or two. It shows others that I'm real, with personal opinions, likes, and dislikes. I steer clear of politics, religion, and anything overtly sexual, though I have strong opinions on those topics. Why? Because while I want to be seen as authentic, I strive to balance that with being professional. As an editor, I couldn't care less about a writer's political or religious viewpoints or sexual orientation. Since my goal is to present a balanced image, I choose to avoid running off potential clients by spouting my views on politics or hopping on one of my many soapboxes.

Remember, it takes time to build your brand. Keep in mind that clients are selecting you from a host of others. Something has to set you apart, especially if you're so busy that you have to ask them to wait months for your services. So be yourself, within reason, and be professional.

Once you've established a client base, things get a little easier, with satisfied clients spreading the word about your editing skills, the ease of communicating with you, and their own willingness to wait for your services when other editors might be available sooner. They'll appreciate how supportive you are on both a personal and professional level as you celebrate their successes and help them mourn their failures along the way. Those clients will also start reserving editing time long before their books are complete, just to be certain they can receive your services when they're ready. It takes some careful scheduling and a hefty dose of flexibility, but I manage to schedule up to one year in advance without many issues arising.

This might sound too good to be true, but it's not. Is my calendar always overflowing with work? Of course not. There have definitely been slowdowns, especially during times of pandemic and high inflation, but things come back around.

No matter how busy you are, there's never time to sit back and rest when it comes to maintaining your sterling reputation. The competition is stiff, and the work is ongoing. What follows are suggestions for keeping yourself two steps ahead of others in your field.

Teach Them What You Know

Writers are a unique breed of individuals. The serious ones are hungry for anything that will help them improve their writing skills. They're like sponges, soaking up everything you have to offer that might make a difference in their skill level. As a former teacher, this is the perfect setup for me. I have an eager, attentive group of "students" who are delighted to learn the skills I have to offer. With self-editing such an important part of the writing process, I have useful information to offer—information that, if absorbed, studied, and used, can encourage writers to come back for more.

Teaching writers what I know about the intricacies of language usage as I edit can be time-consuming. It's so much more than just sticking in the missing commas and correcting misspelled words. I write a lot of comments as I edit. As I explain to my clients, many of these are strictly for the purpose of instruction. How can a writer learn what they're doing wrong if it's not explained to them? There's an art to doing this, so be sure to strive for that professional/real person balance in your comments.

Of course there's always that part of editing that is subjective, where your personal preferences long to creep into the picture. While you have to keep your ego in check, it is okay to show your clients that there are other ways of doing things. Just give them a variety of examples—all accurately written, of course.

It's not unusual for my edits to have hundreds of comments—maybe even 500 or more if the manuscript is long. They're brief, sometimes only one word, but it definitely takes time (there's that word again) to do that. Does it slow me down? Yes. Could I edit for more clients each month if I left out those comments? Yes, I could. But it's not the number of manuscripts you hurry through that makes you worth waiting for; it's the quality of your work and the time you spend polishing your reputation that make the difference.

I had a client post an article via BookDaily.com in which she sang my praises and said I made her a better writer. There's nothing more satisfying than that. An hour after the article was tweeted, I had a new client booked for an edit five months in advance. She'd read the article and wanted to know more about me. She checked out my website, where she perused the client testimonials, and promptly scheduled her edit, paying the $200 deposit I require for advance booking.

The bottom line is all serious writers want to be better at their craft. Teaching my clients how to avoid common and not-so-common errors in their writing empowers them and gives them confidence in their writing skills. That confidence extends directly back to my editing and keeps writers coming back for more. It makes me worth the wait, and I'm proud of that.

Surrender Your Role as Team Captain

This part of the game can be a tough one for me. I have a dominant personality type and am used to being the doer and organizer, which doesn't always work well when a client hands their writing over to me after countless hours of blood, sweat, and tears. To be a wait-worthy editor, you need a reputation as someone who is firm, confident in your editing skills but not pushy or opinionated. I'll admit that I go back over the comments I've written before returning an edit to a client. I make changes if necessary, taking out any snarky-sounding comments or overly pushy advice that might have crept in during the editing process. I am human, after all, and sometimes my hair-pulling creeps into my comments during a difficult edit. I don't want my clients to get a taste of that side of me.

The fact is the work I'm editing isn't mine. I'm not the captain on this team; I'm a key player, but not the primary one. My goal is to return an error-free project to the client, complete with explanations about why I made the changes or suggestions I did, while leaving the writer with the knowledge that they're in control of the project. And they are in control. Since I'm a freelancer, there's no rule that says they have to accept my changes or recommendations. But they pay good money to hire me and wait months for my services, so I'll offer them up in an effort to make each project better than it was when it first crossed my desk.

So, Now What?

In a perfect world, the writer loves what I've done with their work, offers ebullient words of praise, writes a glowing testimonial for my website, and comes back again and again for editing, often booking way ahead to be sure I'm available when they're ready. It does happen that way—frequently enough that I often have trouble finding room for new clients. But this is not a perfect world, and not all clients are the same. There will be plenty of bumps in the road as you strive to position yourself at the top of the freelance editor list, but those obstacles can be handled with grace if you're prepared for them.

Are all clients going to be 100-percent satisfied with your work? No. There will be plenty who are one-timers who disagree with what you've done and take your comments and suggestions as criticism. It happens. Let go of those clients. Keep it professional and resist the temptation to keep communicating with them in order to figure out what you could have done differently. Learn to pick your battles wisely.

Here's my last bit of advice. . . .

Charge What You're Worth

Nothing screams "I'm not really sure I'm any good at this" like charging a dollar a page for your work. If you've been networking on social media, you've seen those offers out there. If you're doing a thorough job of editing, and you're good at it, your time is worth way more than that. Keep in mind that your goal is not to cram as many editing jobs into your schedule as is humanly possible. For the wait-worthy editor, it's about the quality of the work, not the number of low-paying jobs.

I started out charging much less than I do today. It didn't take long for me to figure out that I was doing myself a disservice. I charge by the word for most manuscripts, but it depends upon the client's writing skills and the type of editing required. For some projects, an hourly rate works better. The EFA provides a chart of the range of rates their members receive on their website. If you've never seen it, it's available at the-efa.org/rates.

If you use the reported rates as a guide, you're charging way more than a dollar a page. And guess what? You're worth it! My clients, for the most part, agree. (Remember that thick skin I recommended? You'll be able to put those naysayers aside without a second thought.) They pay my rates—half of the total due before the start date and the remainder, in full, before they ever see a single page of their edited work. I've earned their trust. You can do the same if you're willing to put in some effort.

Don't Overbook

This is a hard one for me, something I've had to make a conscious effort to avoid. I learned the hard way after trying to squeeze in just one more little job in an already cramped schedule. The result was several weeks of working long hours, including weekends, to get everything accomplished. I did it, but I was miserable.

As your client base grows and the word gets out that you're worth waiting for, don't let greed rule the day. (Remember that ego you're keeping in check? Now's the time to practice that.) The money is nice, but if it comes at the expense of your sanity and personal life, it's certainly not worth it. Your work will suffer, as will your reputation.

Clients can always find an "editor" who is available immediately and often at half the cost. At first, I tried hard to fit everyone in. It's just not possible. Now I am rarely able to work people in at the last minute; if they don't want to wait, I'm okay with that. And those potential clients who hurried off to book one of those one-dollar-a-page editors with a two-day turnaround time? They often come back, determined to pay for professional editing and willing to wait several months to get it done right.

In Conclusion

I didn't set out to be a full-time editor. I dabbled in it at first, found I was good at it, and gave it a shot with the encouragement of a writer-friend. I'm slow and meticulous, determined to return every edit in much better shape than when I received it. I moved from actively searching for editing jobs to word-of-mouth referrals from satisfied customers. I take every job seriously and treat each client with the same respect, whether I'm copyediting for a magazine or editing a novel for someone whose books will probably never be on the *New York Times* bestsellers list.

I strive to make a personal connection with my clients, to make them feel more confident in their writing. I can explain every single mark I make on their projects and am willing—eager—to do so. I want to be invaluable to my clients. Sometimes they have other ideas, but the connection is made more often than not. It's terrifying and gratifying and requires some finesse and flexibility, but it's worth it.

I'm worth the wait. You can be too.

About the Author

Susan Hughes is a freelance editor with a wide range of experience. While her first love is working with indie authors, she has edited both fiction and nonfiction, poetry, corporate and education-related publications, and blog posts. Susan is a former editor for *Addison Magazine* and has performed pre-submission editing for a number of clients whose op-ed pieces appeared in *The Huffington Post* and *Fox News Latino*.

Susan earned a BA in English Literature from the University of Houston at Clear Lake and spent 29 years as an educator. She is a member of the Editorial Freelancers Association and ACES: The Society for Editing.

www.ingramcontent.com/pod-product-compliance
Lightning Source LLC
Chambersburg PA
CBHW052211110526
44591CB00012B/2163

Writing to Heal

Carlene Stanislaus

Copyright 2024

All Rights Reserved

No part of this publication may be reproduced, stored in a retrieval system, or transmitted in any form or by any means, electronic, mechanical, photocopying, recording, or otherwise, without the written permission of the author or the publisher.

Contents

Dedication i

Acknowledgements ii

About the Author iii

Inspiration for Writing My Book 1

My Morning Routine 9

Stick Person Representation 11

Introduction 15

Searching 17

Look Within 18

My Message 19

Hope Love Light 20

I Rise 21

Fly With Me 22

The Warrior 23

Transition 24

Path to Glory 25

The Light Within You 26

Dedication

I dedicate this book to My Son Sammy Orlando Bahous who has believed in me throughout my ups and downs in my life. My brother, Marlon Stanislaus, who encouraged me and told me "It's always darkest before dawn." To the CEO of Voices of Hope Kingston who through all their transformative projects in the community led to my poetry being heard at The Pearl Awards in 2022, to my Creative Writing Teacher Richard Neville who encouraged and supported my writing. To you the readers of this book, my heartfelt desire for you is to empower and inspire you to love yourself enough to allow yourself to heal from trauma and abuse by writing to heal.

Acknowledgements

To my Son Sammy who has believed in me throughout my ups and downs in my life. My brother Marlon who has always encouraged and supported me. To the CEO of Voices of Hope Kingston who through all their transformative projects in the community led to my poetry being heard at The Pearl Awards in 2022, to my Creative Writing Teacher Richard Neville who was absolutely brilliant and instrumental in the process of my creative writing. To you, the readers of this book, my heartfelt desire is for you to be empowered and inspired, to love yourself enough to allow yourself time to heal from trauma and abuse by writing to heal. After the healing process commences you begin to see yourself in a new light.

About the Author

Carlene Stanislaus, a devoted mother and certified professional in Life Coaching, mBIT, and NLP, seamlessly integrates spirituality with community service. In the area of the Healing Arts, Carlene has certifications in Angelic Reiki Master Teacher and Usui Reiki Master. These were studied to help with the healing process when they were relevant to her healing journey. Currently enrolled in the Bob Proctor Coaching and Mentoring Program under Sandy Gallagher, she continues the transformative work of the late Bob Proctor. Beyond her certifications, Carlene is a trustee for a local charity and the founder of KIS, a community initiative addressing mental health. Passionate about personal growth, she enjoys singing, dancing, writing, and fitness, all while embracing her faith with love for God.

Inspiration for Writing My Book

Firstly, writing has always been a dream of mine. You know how life goes. You have a number of things you desire to see fulfilled and writing a book gets pushed to the bottom of your to-do list.

So I have decided to make my dream a reality in the hope that something in this book will inspire and encourage you to move forward with your goals and the vision you have for your life. I encourage you to dream and dream big, believe in yourself and surround yourself with at least 5 people who will empower and support you with the vision you have for yourself.

You see, sometimes the things that are near and dear to your heart are the things you need to focus on to catapult you to the next level. With that said I made a decision to take a leap of faith and share some of my journey to date.

If you're hoping to read in these pages that my journey has been full of sunshine and roses, well I have to break it to you now it has not been, however I turned water into wine (Genesis 2:18 -25) I partnered with God in all my endeavours and I allowed him to use me as his instrument to share these words to help those looking for the light and in need of hope.

I am here to tell you that no matter what has happened in your life to never ever give up, even when your physical reality shows that you are in the wilderness remember that "it is always darkest before dawn". In a moment where I questioned my life and the things that I had been through, these were the very words my brother Marlon used to lift me up.

So to you my dear readers of this book always have hope and believe that your pain will one day turn to peace. Your sadness could lead you to your success tomorrow. We are not on this planet by chance or accident, you were created on purpose for a purpose and that's unique just for you. Somewhere someone is waiting for you to show up, and without you they can't fulfil their purpose.

So when you're ready, dry your tears, pick yourself up and go again. Life is what you make of it. "A quitter never wins and winner never quits" - Vince Lombardi. You can choose to focus on loss, limitation and failure or you can see hope, abundance and success and give yourself a chance to be that person whom you were always destined to be underneath the perils of past hurt and suffering. As children of God we are bigger than any problem or circumstance, so this is an opportunity to grow and overcome any disappointments. You owe it to yourself to be the person you were created to be.

What might that look like for you, you may have to go on a personal and professional development training program? Are you willing to do that? If you are willing to put yourself out there to learn and grow you can achieve anything you want, you've just to go be willing to give it your best effort.

By now you're probably wondering how to change your life, how do you turn things around and make them better? Well most people tend to put things off for sometime in the future, I will do "X" when "Y" happens - you know that old chestnut, when the kids get older I will take action, when I see the money I will commit and do that thing.

I used to be like that, however two close friends of mine recently passed to Spirit and what I learnt from them were these two things:

1. Do whatever makes you happy, worry less about what others think and want you to do for them or to make them happy.
2. Make your dreams and goals your priority because tomorrow is not promised

My friends were in their 80's. They still had things on their list they wanted to accomplish however they put them off until sometime in the future. They didn't manage to complete them here on earth, perhaps they are completing them in the After Life, who knows?

If you are a giver like me, you can find yourself always giving and finding yourself with not enough time for your needs. So here's the key if you don't already know this - be the star in your own movie and not a supporting player in your life. No one is going to tell you to put yourself first, so you need to take charge to create the life you want by leading yourself towards the desires of your heart, to do whatever else makes you feel happy. At the end of the day you only get one life right!! If you're not already putting you at the top of your list then I strongly recommend you start putting you first and watch and see what happens.

I started putting myself first, investing large sums of money into myself, I started going to the gym with my son, along with following a winning morning routine which sets me up for my day and the week ahead. (I will share my morning routine with you later in this book). I can truly say that I have experienced a massive shift in my outlook, my perception of my life and my results. Even to write this book and to get it ready to be published. My morning routine has been a massive help to shifting my old paradigm and shifting my mindset to move me past limitations to endless possibilities.

Take a look at the world around us, we are often subject to information overload. We allow what's going on outside to control what's going on inside. That's the way many people are living their lives today.

I decided to write this book to help you my dear reader to do something different to what you have already done in order to transform your life and see yourself through a different lens. At times our perception of who we are and what we are capable of can be tainted by our past experiences, patterns and behaviour (paradigm), and the way in which we see ourselves.

Here are a few tips I'd like to share to help you to change and be that person whom you were ordained to be. I invite you to try them if any of them resonate with you.

1. Morning Routine - Morning routines build you up and strengthen your belief and your confidence in yourself.
2. Gratitude - Gratitude is a fundamental part of life, give thanks for all your blessings and where you are at this very moment. It may not seem like it depending on what you're dealing with currently. It is my belief that everything happens just as it's supposed to, there are no coincidences, nothing happens by chance. When you are grateful for what you have, you open the door to receiving more of what you are grateful for.
3. Self Image - Create a strong self image of the person whom you desire to be. A winning image.
4. Invest - Invest in yourself to assist you on your journey of personal growth and self mastery.
5. Exercise - Exercise strengthens your body and your mind, make this part of your weekly regime.
6. Decisions - Decide what you want to do with your life, who you want to become, where are you going and how you will get there. (If you don't, someone else will decide for you).

7. Goals - Set your goals and take daily action steps towards achieving your goals.

8. Mindset - Develop a success mindset, mindset will get you closer to where you want to be, as everything is first created in your mind until it manifests itself into your physical reality. So ensure to use your mind to cultivate your desired results.

9. Talking - Talking Therapy, talking to someone whom you are comfortable with and sharing what's in your heart especially if it's weighing you down can be very valuable to your healing journey, you may prefer a counsellor. Do what you feel comfortable with as we are all different, what works for me may not work for you.

10. Environment - The environment you're in is very important, surround yourself with well mannered positive people who encourage your happiness, growth and fulfilment.

11. Reading - Reading is a fundamental part of your growth, it's essential to study the lives of those who are going where you want to go or have an understanding of what you have gone through/are going through in your life. Leaders are readers, if you are an adult you are a leader. You will need to lead yourself through your daily life. Aside from that reading may be a great

way for you to learn, unwind, relax and create meaning for you and your loved ones.

12. Celebrate - Celebrate where you are now in your life, and where you want to go. Celebrate every win, large or small.

13. Joy - Find the things that bring you joy and enjoy them as often as you can. Have fun and play - this raises your vibration and can create space for creative energy to flow in and through you.

14. Love - Love yourself enough to say yes to you first and no to the things which bring you down. Make time to share your life with those whom you love dearly and to do things you love often.

15. Forgiveness - Forgive yourself for anything you may have conspired to, knowingly or unknowingly. Forgive anyone who has hurt you in the past. In forgiving you release yourself from any past hurt, anger and resentment. This then creates a space for you to heal and move on from the past. This will allow you to harness your creativity and maximise your awesome potential which may be laying dormant, as a result of unforgiveness.

When your heart is full of unforgiveness you can very often feel blocked, stuck, lost and in need of clarity. This can also manifest itself in your mind and body and lead to dis-ease. I encourage you to release all that no longer serves you, and allow yourself to fully heal.

16. Giving - Everything you give comes back to you multiplied, if you are in a position to give something of value to uplift others it will help you to see just how valuable you are. Even if it's a small thing, small things are big things, especially when you are not at your best. Your giving could transform someone's perception of themselves and their life in that moment.

    You could give time by volunteering (giving back to your community), money, unwanted items, clothes, books, jewellery ect. When you give you're creating a harmonious, peaceful energy exchange between you and that individual or organisation.

    It is my belief that we are all here to serve/help each other somehow in some form, some where. Give whatever you are happy to give. You also make space for you to receive. "Give and it shall be given unto you". (Luke 6:38).

My Morning Routine

I use the following morning routine to set me up for the day and the week ahead.

1. Prayer - Pray to whatever deity you are accustomed to praying to, (only do this if praying resonates with you).

2. Gratitude - Write out 10 things you are grateful for, these can include things you have now and things you expect to receive. Examples: I am so happy and grateful for my beautiful home, I am so happy and grateful for my holiday to Spain in summer 2024 etc.

3. Write out your goals, 3 times in the morning, 6 times in the afternoon and 9 times at night. When you write out your goals several times, the following happens :

- Writing causes Thinking,
- Thinking creates an Image,
- Images control Feelings,
- Feelings cause Actions,
- Actions create Results

4. Autosuggestion - Autosuggestion (means a suggestion from yourself to yourself). This tool is very powerful for influencing the subconscious mind. Auto suggest your goals each day for peak performance and productivity. Autosuggest your goals for about 5/10 minutes each day.

5. Affirmations - Write out your affirmations daily 10 or more. You can also auto-suggest your affirmations by saying them out loud. This has a powerful effect on your subconscious mind.

6. I am statements - Write out 10 I am statements and auto suggest them. Example: I am talented, I am valuable, I am more than enough etc.

7. Visualisation - Spend at least 10 - 15 minutes visualising yourself becoming the person you want to be. See yourself achieving your goals and celebrating that they are already done.

8. Meditation - Meditate for 10 - 20 minutes, just relax and if there are questions you require answers to, these can come to you intuitively during your meditation.

Stick Person Representation

The Mind

Before I conclude my book I wanted to include some information which I sincerely hope will be valuable to enable you to use your mind to obtain your desired outcomes.

Now whilst on a Coaching and Mentoring Program I discovered from my Mentors Bob Proctor & Sandy Gallagher of Proctor Gallagher Institute just how powerful the mind really is. (Bob Proctor - passed to spirit on 3 Feb 2022). His legacy lives on!

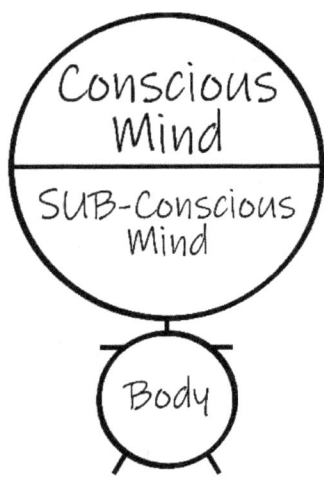

The diagram is called the Stick Person and it was created by Dr Thurman Fleet in 1934, from San Antonio Texas

When we think of the mind we may get an image of the brain or nothing at all. You see the thing is, no one has ever seen the mind so describing the mind can be very challenging. Luckily for us a gentleman by the name of Dr Thurman Fleet from San Antonio, Texas created the above diagram as his representation of the mind in 1934.

This representation of the mind for me is clear, easy to understand and articulate. The mind is the greatest power there is, the way we use our mind will dictate what we attract into our lives. Let me break this information down into more manageable chunks.

The top circle in the diagram is drawn considerably bigger, this is for a very good reason. You see, the mind is extremely powerful. The second circle at the bottom of the diagram represents the body and is much smaller.

The top half of the big circle represents the conscious mind. This is the part of the mind where we gather information, pile up all the knowledge and everything we learn. This is sometimes known as the thinking mind. The conscious mind can accept or reject information. The conscious mind can also originate ideas. The Conscious mind is also known as the intellectual mind. Our Intellectual Faculties reside in our conscious mind. Our Intellectual Faculties are: Imagination, Memory, Reason, Perception, Intuition and Will. Our sensory faculties are also hooked up to our conscious mind, like antennas. Our thoughts good or bad, lack and limitations originate in our conscious mind.

The bottom half of the big circle represents the Subconscious mind - this is known as the feeling mind or the emotional mind. This is the most powerful part of the mind. Your subconscious mind has to accept whatever you impress upon it, it has no ability to reject whatever information you give to it.

This means that any thoughts you impress upon your subconscious mind repeatedly will become fixed within your subconscious mind. Therefore it is imperative to ensure that the thoughts you impress upon your mind are positive for you. Whatever is impressed upon your subconscious mind must be expressed through the body. Through your feelings and your actions.

This is a huge game changer. We can often obtain various qualifications by gathering lots of information, however utilising what we have learnt is often a problem. When you learn how to use your subconscious mind this will no longer be an issue.

When I started to understand just what a powerhouse the subconscious mind is, that was a massive aha moment for me. I do hope that you will use your powerful mind to achieve the outstanding results you seek. You'll be amazed at just what's possible for you.

Last but not least is the body, the body is the small circle at the bottom of the large circle (the mind). The body is the instrument of the mind. Whatever you impress upon your subconscious mind must be expressed with and through the body and will show up in your actions and ultimately affect your results.

I will leave you with a few closing words, in all that we do with our day to day lives. I encourage you to study yourself, in studying yourself you get to understand you. Why you are the way you are, why you do the things you do. Once you understand you, you are then better equipped to understand others. You owe it yourself to become the best version of you.

I dared to dream and the results are the manifestation of this book.

Dream big and go where your heart calls you, you are meant to live in freedom, love and joy. I really hope you accomplish all your heart's desires.

With love and very best wishes.

Carlene X

Introduction

All healing has to come firstly from the person who requires the healing, this involves letting go and allowing oneself to be vulnerable, in a safe space to heal and let go of what no longer serves them.

There are no judgments, if we are willing to let go of the hurt and pain and start the healing journey we can expect positive results. Of course I can only speak from my own experience, perception and my journey. Each individual will have to assess their situation and establish what is best for them and take the necessary steps to heal. All healing has a process, I invite you to give yourself into the process and begin your journey.

As you embark on your healing journey it is possible you may feel the hurt and the pain in your heart as you recall the events on that past timeline, whatever memories which come up for you, allow them to come forward. Any triggers which come to the surface can be dealt with in a manner that suits you. You were that person who encountered these things, in the here and now you will have to release it and let go, to allow yourself to heal. By carrying unhealed trauma in you, from my experience it stifles your creativity and growth. In some instances it can hold you back and keep you in a disempowered state.

Whilst struggling with the adversities in my life, I started writing poetry and I discovered through writing, that I was able to let go of some of the things which had strongholds over me. Writing enabled me to remove some of the adverse effects of what I had endured throughout my life hence the title of this book "Writing to Heal".

I cannot promise that writing will help everyone to heal, what I can say about writing is that it allows you the freedom to extract some of the imprints of what you have been through in your life so far. Essentially liberating you to let it all go and free yourself from past pain and suffering, to then implant newness and freshness to create what you truly desire.

Searching

When things get tough and I feel lost
My soul seeks solace and peace
Where is my solace?
Where is my peace?
I search within
At times there's nothing there

I wander and I roam
I look to those of influence, power, poise and prolific positions
World leaders, teachers, mentors and high-profile influencers
Heralded as great
They impact the world

Who are they?
Strip back the layers, the garments adorned, the lifestyles portrayed

It goes further, deeper and beyond

So while we look up to world leaders and we follow
these so called iconic influencers
Let us go deeper
And see what we discover
Search your heart, search your soul
Know thyself
When it's all said and done
That's the ultimate goal

Look Within

Look within
You'll see your greatness
Your hidden treasure
No man can measure
You were born great
You're a perfect gifting

Now is the time to see your light
You're a perfect creation
You shine so bright
Unshackle the chains
Unbreak the ties that bind

Walk in your beauty
Walk in your light
All veils are lifted
Your search has now ended

The solace and peace
You used to seek
Resides way down deep
Way down deep inside of you
The leader you seek
Was always in you

My Message

Abused and bullied by those I trusted
Confused, manipulated, lost and afraid
That's how they left me
The narcissist will live with their guilt eroding their life and conscious

Triggered and traumatised by my past
These things I couldn't control
Grief loss and depression
All play their part in my journey

So what now
It's okay
Cos I've got this
My life means so much more
Than what has gone before
And all the things I've had to endure

I weathered the storms
And I'm still here
I'm still here
I'm going to keep on keeping on
With life, breath and God beside me
I am rising up and I will overcome
I will always fight for me

Hope Love Light

You see that abused and bullied little girl she's gone

No longer am I oppressed, suppressed or depressed

I have triumphed over the trials and tribulations of my life

I am liberated and free to live my life sharing a new story

I am my message of hope, love, light, kindness, joy and glory.

I am my message, I'm not my mess

I Rise

Out of the dust I take form
Out of the dust like the phoenix, my flame burns bright
In the darkest night my flame radiates hues of yellow, orange, red and white

In the distant sky my light illuminates the sky at night
Like the stars in the sky I'm high
With all the power in my soul
And the divine essence in my spirit
Like the phoenix I rise
I rise

Fly With Me

Come fly with me
I'm going to take you on a journey
It's okay to close your eyes and trust me
It's okay to journey far and wide and just be
Don't be afraid to explore
There are times in life when you have to leave the shore

The Warrior

I stand tall and strong
Confident that I can withstand the storm
I will prevail
I will overcome

Transition

I am not my past, I am not my future
In this present moment I flow with life
And I allow things to be
I am always learning and growing in confidence, each and every day
My healing and growth is a process
I am no longer who I used to be
I am not yet who I want to be
In this now moment
I accept the transitional version of me

Path to Glory

Let the light of your soul lift you up to the highest high, your soul knows the truth

Walk in the light of this truth for there lies all the answers which you seek

The light of your soul will illuminate your path and take you to your rightful destination

Trust the light of your soul and know the light of your soul has no secrets to hide from you

The light of your soul now fully awakened to all it's truth can never be dimmed in darkness

The light of your soul is your calling card to happiness, fulfillment and the freedom you seek

It is now time to walk in the light

The light of your soul

The Light Within You

Your spark
Your essence
Your beingness
Your brilliance
Transforms your world
Do not dim your light to fit in
You incarnated on this earth with a clear blue print of what you will co - create with God/Source
To help heal and soothe your soul and thus, when you first heal from your wounds you help to heal many others around you too.
You tell the story
You wear the scars of survival
Open your heart to heal
Open your heart to love
So walk now in love
Walk now in light
Fill your soul with eternal love and and light
Rise up and be the light bearer
The time is now
Humanity is calling and this is your calling
As you lead the way for yourself
You uplift and inspire your earthly brothers and sisters to take heed
To step forward
To step up
And honour their truths
To trust
To listen
To answer the call of their soul

www.ingramcontent.com/pod-product-compliance
Lightning Source LLC
Chambersburg PA
CBHW052210110526
44591CB00012B/2159